Alan Gray, J. M. (John Mason) Neale

A Song Of Redemption

Alan Gray, J. M. (John Mason) Neale

A Song Of Redemption

ISBN/EAN: 9783741156175

Manufactured in Europe, USA, Canada, Australia, Japa

Cover: Foto ©Angelika Wolter / pixelio.de

Manufactured and distributed by brebook publishing software
(www.brebook.com)

Alan Gray, J. M. (John Mason) Neale

A Song Of Redemption

HANDEL

NOVELLO'S ORIGINAL OCTAVO EDITION

ALAN GRAY.

A

SONG OF REDEMPTION

ONE SHILLING & SIXPENCE.

75c

THE CATHEDRAL
PARAGRAPH PSALTER

CONTAINING THE

CANTICLES, PSALMS, AND PROPER PSALMS

ARRANGED IN PARAGRAPHS AND POINTED FOR CHANTING

TOGETHER WITH

A SCHEME OF APPROPRIATE CHANTS AND BRIEF NOTES ON THE PSALTER

EDITED BY THE

REV. J. TROUTBECK, D.D.

(Chaplain in Ordinary to the Queen and Precentor of Westminster).

PRICE THREE SHILLINGS AND SIXPENCE.

The principle of Pointing followed is that of the Cathedral Psalter, with slight modifications here and there, suggested by experience, in the treatment of individual verses. For the accents which are used in the Cathedral Psalter to indicate the beginning of the bar of duple time, which connects the free recitation with the metrical part of the chant, are substituted super-imposed musical notes, in accordance with the principle set forth in the Preface to the Cathedral Psalter, so as to indicate exactly, in every verse throughout the Psalter, the best method of dividing the bar into the component parts of a semibreve. Other means also have been adopted to ensure clearness and promote facility

Prefixed to the new Psalter is a Scheme of Chants and some brief Notes on the History of the Psalter and the Characteristics of each Psalm.

THIRD EDITION (REVISED AND GREATLY ENLARGED).

Containing 600 Chants. Price 2s. 6d.; Cloth, 3s.

THE WESTMINSTER ABBEY CHANT BOOK

ARRANGED AND EDITED BY THE

REV. J. TROUTBECK, D.D.
(Chaplain in Ordinary to the Queen and Minor Canon of Westminster),

AND

J. FREDERICK BRIDGE, Mus. Doc.

(Organist of Westminster Abbey and Gresham Professor of Music).

This Edition has been arranged in connection with the CATHEDRAL PARAGRAPH PSALTER, prepared by Dr. Troutbeck on the lines of the Cathedral Psalter.

It has been enriched by many fresh contributions, including Single, Double, and Triple Chants—specially written for the Psalms to which they are set—by Dr. J. F. Bridge, J. Foster, Myles B. Foster, Dr. G. M. Garrett, Battison Haynes, Dr. A. C. Mackenzie, John E. West, Dr. G. C. Martin, Sir Herbert Oakeley, Sir John Stainer, B. Tours, and others, besides many now printed for the first time, by Sir Joseph Barnby, H. Smart, &c.

LONDON & NEW YORK: NOVELLO, EWER AND CO.

NOVELLO'S ORIGINAL OCTAVO EDITION.

COMPOSED FOR THE LEEDS MUSICAL FESTIVAL, 1898.

A

SONG OF REDEMPTION

THE VERSE WRITTEN BY

THE REV. J. M. NEALE

THE MUSIC COMPOSED FOR

SOPRANO SOLO, CHORUS, AND ORCHESTRA

BY

ALAN GRAY.

PRICE ONE SHILLING AND SIXPENCE.

LONDON: NOVELLO AND COMPANY, LIMITED
AND
NOVELLO, EWER AND CO., NEW YORK.

LONDON:
NOVELLO AND COMPANY, LIMITED.
PRINTERS.

A SONG OF REDEMPTION.

I.

Allegro maestoso. 𝅗𝅥 = *about* 88.

ALAN GRAY.

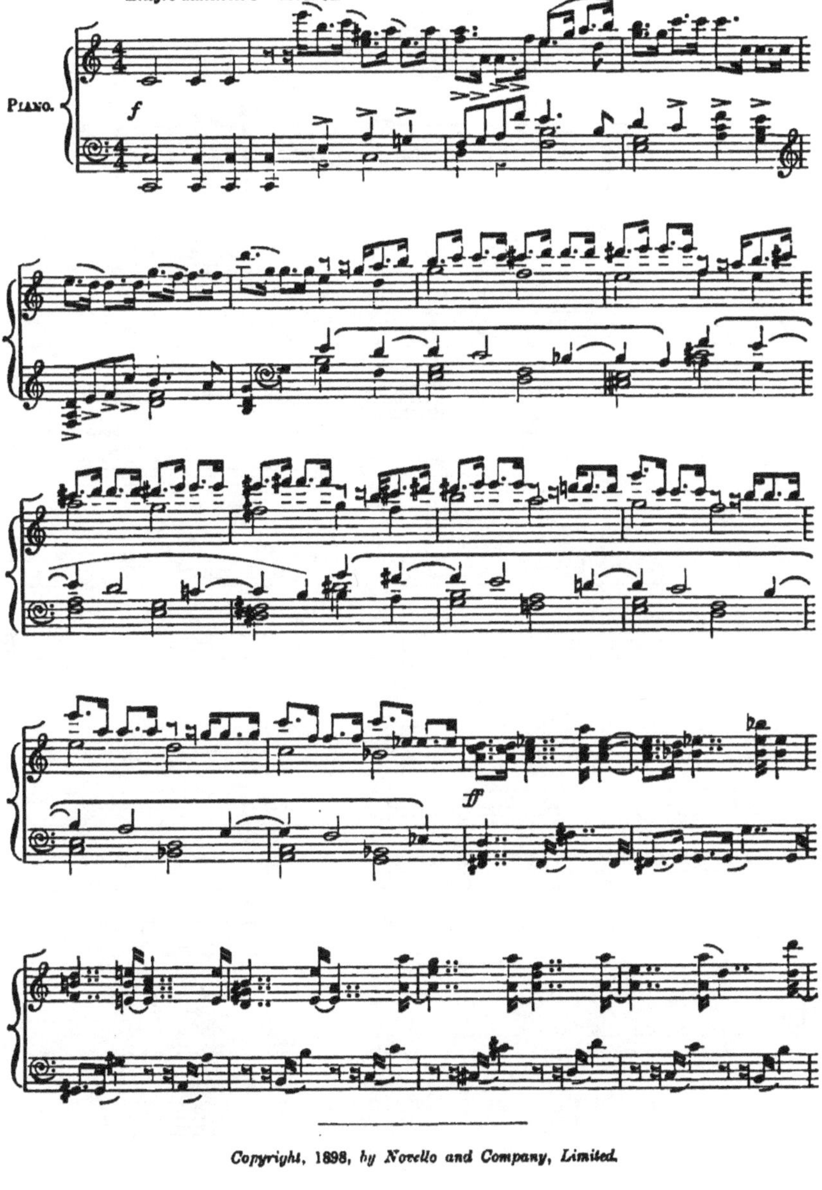

Soprano. A
The foe be - hind, the deep be - fore, ...

Alto.
The foe be - hind, the deep be - fore, . . . Our

Tenor.
The foe be - hind, the deep be - fore, Our hosts have

Bass.
The foe be - hind, the deep be - fore, . . . Our

. . . Our hosts have dared and passed the sea,

hosts have dared and passed the sea, our

dared and passed, and passed the sea,

hosts have dared and passed the sea, The foe be

3

8234

shore, and Pharoah's war-riors strew . . . . the

and Pharoah's war-riors strew, . . strew . . . . the

Pharoah's war-riors strew the shore, the war - riors

shore, and Pha-roah's war- riors, Pha-roah's war-riors

shore, ... And Is - rael's ran -somed tribes are free,

shore, ... And Is - rael's ran -somed tribes are free,

strew the shore, And Is - rael's ran-somed tribes are free,

strew the shore, And Is - rael's ran -somed tribes are free,

and Is - rael's ran - somed tribes are free, ...

and Is - rael's ran - somed tribes are free, ...

and Is - rael's ran - somed tribes are free, ...

and Is - rael's ran - somed tribes are free, ...

SOPRANO SOLO.

Lift up, lift up your voi - ces

are free.

are free.

are free.

are free.

mf *p*

now! The whole wide world .. re - joi - ces now!

pp

The Lord . . . hath triumphed glo - rious-ly,

the Lord hath tri - umphed glo - rious-ly :

6

The Lord shall reign, . . . shall reign . . . vic - to - - - rious-

colla voce.

C

- ly !

Chorus.

The foe be - hind, the deep be - fore, Our hosts have

The foe be - hind, the deep be - fore, Our hosts have

The foe be - hind, the deep be - fore, Our hosts have dared and

The foe be - hind, the deep be - fore, . Our hosts . . have

C

f a tempo.

dared and passed the sea. . our hosts, . .

dared and passed the sea, our hosts have

passed . . the sea, The foe be - hind, the deep be -

dared and passed the sea, The foe be - hind, the deep be - -

8234.

. . our hosts have dared and passed the sea : . . . . And Pha -
dared . . and passed the sea : The foe be -
- fore, Our hosts have dared and passed the sea : The foe be -
- fore, the foe be - hind, the deep be -
- - roah's war - riors strew . . . the . . shore, strew . .
- hind, the deep be - fore, Our hosts have dared and passed the sea, . . have
- hind, the deep be - fore, Our hosts have dared and passed the sea, our hosts have
- fore, Our hosts have dared and passed the sea, our hosts have dared and passed the
. the shore, . . And Is - rael's ran - somed tribes, Is - rael's ransomed
dared and passed the sea : And Is - rael's ran - somed tribes, . . Is - rael's ransomed
dared and passed the sea : And Is - rael's ran - somed tribes, . . Is - rael's ransomed
sea : And Is - - rael's ran - somed tribes, Is - rael's ransomed

tribes are free.

tribes are free.

tribes are free.

tribes are free.

sempre ff

dim.

p

mf

II. *Allegretto ma non troppo.* ♩. = 132.

mf

f

SOPRANO.
mf

Hap - py, hap - py mor - row, Turn ing

ALTO.
mf

Hap - py, hap - py mor - row, Turn ing

sor - row In - to peace and mirth! Hap - py mor - row,

sor - row In - to peace and mirth! Turn - ing

Turn - ing sor - row In - to peace . . and

sor - row, turn - ing sor - row In - to peace . . and

mirth!

mirth! Bond - age end - ing, Love de - scend ing O'er . . . the

Bond - age end - ing, Love de - scend - ing O'er . . . the

earth!

earth!

Seals . . . . . as - sur - ing, Guards . . . se-

Seals as - sur . . . . . . ing, Guards se - cur - - -

- cur - ing, Watch . . . His earth-ly prison: Seals are

- - ing, Watch . . . His earth-ly prison: Seals are

Guards are scattered,

shattered, Guards are scattered, Christ .

shattered, Christ .

Hap - - - py mor - row, Turn - ing
Hap - - - py mor - row, Turn - ing
. . hath risen! Hap - - - py mor - row, Turn - ing
. . hath risen! Hap - - - py mor - row, Turn - ing
Solo.
Hap - - - py mor - row, Turn - ing sor - row,
sor - - - row In - to peace . . . and mirth,
sor - row . . In - to peace . . . and mirth, . . .
sor - row . . In - to peace . . . and mirth, . . .
sor - row . . In - to peace . . . and mirth, . . .
dim.
p

cres.
p
turn - - - - - ing sor - row In - to
cres.
Turn - ing sor - row, turn - ing sor - row In - to
... Turn - - - - - ing sor - row In - to
... Turn - - - - - ing sor - row In - to
... in - - - - - - - - - to
peace . . . . and mirth!
Andante. 𝅗𝅥 = 104.
p
peace, . . in - to peace . . . and mirth!
pp
peace, . . in - to peace . . . and mirth!
pp
peace, . . in - to peace . . and mirth!
pp
peace . . . . and mirth!
pp
Andante. 𝅗𝅥 = 104.
sempre col Ped.

III.

No long - - er must the mourn - ers weep,

no long - - er must the mourn - ers weep, Nor call . .

p
. . de-part-ed Chris-tians dead, nor call . . de-part-ed
p
F
Chris-tians dead;
p dolce.
col. Ped.
p
For death . . . . is hal-lowed
in to sleep. And ev . . . . 'ry
cres.
f
grave, and ev - - - - - - - 'ry . .
mf

grave . . be - comes a bed.
p
mf
cres.
dim.
rall.
pp
G
Più animato. ♩ = 126.
Chorus. Tenor.
mf cres.
Now, once more, E - den's door O - pen stands . . to mor - tal
Bass.
mf cres.
Now, once more, E - den's door O - pen stands . . to mor - tal
f
G Più animato. ♩ = 126.
p
Chorus. Soprano.
mf cres.
Now, once more, E - den's door
Alto.
mf cres.
Now, once more, E - den's door
eyes,
eyes,
p

O - pen stands . . to mor - tal eyes, ...
O - pen stands . . to mor - tal eyes, ...
Now, once more, E - den's door O - - pen stands,
Now, once more, E - den's door
sempre cres.
o pen stands to mor - tal eyes:
o - pen stands to mor - tal eyes:
o pen stands to mor - tal eyes:
o - pen stands to mor - tal eyes:

ad lib.
f
For Christ hath
fff
risen,
p
f
ad lib.
f
for Christ hath risen,
p a tempo.
Adagio.
Christ hath risen, and man . . . shall
Adagio.
p

IV.

Allegro. ♩ = 69.

rise.

CHORUS.

Now at last . . Old things past, Hope and joy and peace be-

Now at last . Old things past, Hope and joy and peace be-

Now at last . Old things past, Hope and joy and peace be-

Now at last Old things past, Hope and joy and peace be-

Allegro. ♩ = 69.

f

- gin : For Christ hath won, and man shall

- gin : For Christ hath won, hath won, and man shall

- gin : For Christ hath won, Christ hath won, and man shall

For Christ hath won, for Christ hath won,

win,

win,

win,

Now at last . . Old things past, Hope and joy and peace be-

For Christ hath won, and man shall win,

For Christ hath won, for Christ hath won, Now at last . .

For Christ hath won, and man shall win,

- gin, For Christ hath won, and man shall win,

Now at last Old things

Old things past, old things past, now. now . at

Now at last . Old things past, now . . . at

Now at last . Old things past, . .

past, Hope and joy and peace be - gin, hope and joy and peace be -

last, Hope and joy and peace be - gin, hope and joy and peace be -

last, Hope and joy and peace be - gin, hope and joy and peace be -

Now at last, . . hope and joy be -

gin, hope and joy and peace be - gin
gin, hope and joy and peace be - gin:
gin, hope and joy and peace be - gin:
gin, hope and joy and peace be - gin:
8va
Now at last . . . Old things past, Hope and
Now at last . . Old things past, Hope and
Now at last . Old things past, old things past, Hope and
Now at last Old things past, now . . at last, Hope and
joy and peace be - gin: For Christ . . hath won, and
joy and peace be - gin: For Christ . . hath won, and
joy and peace be - gin: For Christ . . hath won, and
joy and peace be - gin: For Christ . . hath won, and

man shall win.

man shall win.

man shall win.

man shall win.

sempre ff

Ped.

col 8vi.　*Ped.*

22

8284.

Andante sostenuto.
high. . . .
Andante sostenuto. ♩= 56.
pp
f
It is not sad - ness, peace from strife, . . it is . . not
sad - ness, it is not sad - ness, peace, peace from strife:
dolce.
p
To fall . . a - sleep . . is
not . . to die, to fall, . to fall . . a -

sleep is not .. to die: To

dwell with Christ, to .. dwell with Christ, to dwell with Christ is ..

bet - ter life, to dwell with Christ to .. dwell with Christ is

life, . . . is .. life, to dwell with Christ is bet - ter

Allegro maestoso.
life.
Allegro maestoso. ♩ = 66.
f
tr
ff
tr
M
Basses. marcato.
With loins up-girt and
staff in hand, And hast - y mien, and san-dall'd feet, A-round the Pas - chal

Tenors.
With loins up-girt, and
Feast we stand, And of the Pas - - chal Lamb we eat, With loins up -
dim.
f
staff in hand, And hast - y mien and sandall'd feet, A - round the Pas - chal
- girt, and staff in hand, And hast - y mien and sandall'd feet, A -
Altos.
With loins up-girt, and
Feast we stand, And of the Pas - - chal Lamb we eat, With loins up -
- round the Paschal Feast we stand, And of the Pas - chal Lamb we eat, With
f

staff in hand, And hast - y mien and sandall'd feet, A-round the Pas - chal
- girt, and staff in hand, And hast y mien and sandall'd feet, A -
loins up - girt, and san - dall'd feet, A - round . . . the
N
Feast we stand, And of the Pas - - chal Lamb we eat,
- round the Paschal Feast we stand, And of the Pas - chal Lamb we eat,
Pas - chal Feast, And of the Pas-chal Lamb we eat,
N
Sopranos.
With loins up-girt, and
Basses.
With

staff in hand, And hast - y mien and sandall'd feet,

Altos.

With

Tenors.

With loins up girt, and

loins up-girt, and staff in hand, And hast - y mien, and sandall'd feet, A - -

A - round the

loins up-girt, And hast - y mien and san - dall'd feet, A - round the

staff in hand, And hast - y mien and san-dall'd feet, A - round the

- round . . the Feast . . we stand, a - round the

legato.

Pas - chal Feast . . we stand, And of the Pas - chal

Pas - chal Feast . . we stand, And of the Pas - chal

Pas - chal Feast . . we stand, And of the Pas - chal

Pas - chal Feast we stand, And of the Pas - chal

dim.
Lamb we eat,
pp
and of the Pas - chal
Lamb we eat,
and of the Pas - chal
Lamb we eat,
and of the Pas - chal
Lamb we eat,
and of the Pas - chal
dim.
pp
Lamb we eat,
P
Lamb we eat,
Lamb we eat,
Lamb we eat,
p
8ves ad lib.
ff
With loins up-girt, and
With loins up-girt, and
With loins up-girt, and
With loins up-girt, and
cres.
ff

staff in hand, And hast-y mien and san-dall'd feet, A-

staff in hand, And hast-y mien and san-dall'd feet, A-round the Pas - chal

staff in hand, And hast-y mien and san-dall'd feet, A-

staff in hand, And hast-y mien and san-dall'd feet, A-round the Pas - chal

- round the Pas - - chal Feast we stand, a - round the Feast we stand, a-

Feast we stand, a - round the Feast we stand, a-

- round the Pas - chal Feast, a - round the Pas-chal Feast we stand, a-

Feast we stand, a - round, a - round the Pas-chal Feast we stand, a-

- round the Pas - chal Feast.. we stand,

- round the Pas - chal Feast we stand,

- round the Pas - chal Feast.. we stand,

- round the Pas - chal Feast we stand,

And of the Pas - chal Lamb . . . we

And of the Pas - chal Lamb . . . we

And of the Pas - chal Lamb . . . we

And of the Pas - chal Lamb . . . we

VII. *Allegro grazioso.*

So . . . . . shall He col - lect us, di -

eat.

eat.

eat.

eat.

Allegro grazioso. ♩ = 120.

- rect us, pro - tect us, From E - gypt's strand;

So . . . . shall He pre - cede us, and

feed us, and lead us To Ca - - - naan's land.

Più animato.

Toils and foes as - sail - ing,

Più animato.

friends quail - ing, hearts fail - ing, Shall

threat . . . . . in vain,

. Toils and foes as - sail - ing,

friends quail - ing, hearts fail - ing, Shall

threat in vain, shall threat . . . . in

vain:

p a tempo.
If . .
p ad lib.
a tempo.
. . . He be pro - vid - ing, pro - vid - ing, pre - sid - ing, and guid - ing, and
guid - - - - - - - - - - - - - ing To Him, . . . to Him a -
gain.
So . . . . shall He pre -
CHORUS.
1st SOPRANO.
So . . . shall He pre - cede us, and feed us, and lead . . us,
2nd SOPRANO.
So . . . shall He pre - cede us, and feed us, and lead . . us,
1st ALTO.
So . . . shall He pre - cede us, and feed us, and lead us,
2nd ALTO.
So . . . shall He pre - cede us, and feed us, and lead us,

- cede .... us,   pre - cede us,

so .... shall He pre - cede us,   and

so   shall   He pre - cede   us,   and

so   shall   He pre - cede   us,   and

so   shall   He pre - cede   us,   and

cres.

and feed   us, and   guide   us,

feed   us,   pre - cede   and   guide   us,   so . . .

feed   us,   pre - cede   and   guide   us, . .   so . .

feed   us,   and   guide   us, . .   so . .

feed   us,   pre - cede   us,   so

and guide . . us.

. . shall He pre - cede . . us.

shall He guide us.

shall He guide us.

shall He guide us.

Andante sostenuto e tranquillo. ♩ 60.

col Ped.

8284.

più p
dim.
pp
pp
rall.
Ped.
Allegro
Solo.
Christ our
Allegro. ♩ = 104.
Lead - er,
Mon - arch,
Plead - er,
In - ter - ced - er,
Praise . . we and a -

S *mf*

-dore : Ex - ult - - a - tion,

ven - er - a - tion, gra - tu - la - tion,

Bring-ing ev - er - more, *cres.* Ex - ult - a - tion,

ven - er - a - tion, ex - ult - a - tion, ven - er - a - tion,

gra - tu - la - tion, Bring - - - - - ing ev - er -

VIII.

Andante sostenuto e maestoso. ♩ = 69.

— mere.

CHORUS.

Where our ban-ner leads.. us We .. may safe-ly go.

Where our ban-ner leads.. us We may safe-ly go.

Where our ban-ner leads us We .. may safe-ly go.

Where our ban-ner leads.. us We may safe-ly go.

S mf
dore: Ex - ult - - a - tion,
ven - er - a - tion, gra - tu - la - tion,
Bring-ing ev - er - more, Ex - ult - a - tion,
ven - er-a - tion, ex - ult - a - tion, ven - er a - tion,
gra - tu - la - tion, Bring - - - - - - - ing ev - er -
cres.

sempre cres.

- more, bring - - ing ev - - - - -

sempre cres.

- - - - - - - - - er - -

f *rall.*

VIII.

Andante sostenuto e maestoso. ♩ = 69.

- mere.

Chorus.

Where our ban - ner leads .. us We .. may safe - ly go.

Where our ban - ner leads .. us We may safe - ly go.

Where our ban - ner leads us We .. may safe - ly go.

Where our ban - ner leads .. us We may safe - ly go.

Andante sostenuto e maestoso. ♩ = 69.

tr *tr*

Where our Chief pre - cedes us, We .. may face the foe,

Where our Chief pre - cedes us, We may face the foe, we..

Where our Chief pre - cedes us, We may face the foe, we..

Where our Chief pre - cedes us, We may face the foe,

we . . may, we may face . . . . . . the foe.

. . . . may, . . may face the foe, the foe.

. . . . may, . . may face the foe, the foe.

we . . . . may face the foe. His right Arm is

His right Arm is o'er us, His right

o'er us, His right . . . Arm is o'er us, He will guide . us

His right Arm is o'er us, His right . .

. . . Arm is o'er . . . us, He will guide . . . us,

through, He . . will . . guide us through, He will guide . .

8ves ad lib.

His right Arm is o'er us, His right . . . .

Arm is o'er us, He will guide . . . us . . through, will . .

guide . . us through, He will . . . guide us, guide us, He . will

. . . . us through, . . He will . . guide . . . us,

Arm, His . . Arm is o'er us, is . . o'er us, He will guide, will

. . . guide us through, will . . guide . . . us, His right Arm is

guide . . . us through, guide . . . us through, His

He . . . will guide us, guide . . us, His right . . . .

guide . . . . us .. through, will guide . . . . us ..

o'er us, His right . . . Arm is o'er us, He will .. guide ..

right Arm is o'er us, His right Arm is o'er us, His

. . . Arm is o'er . . . us, His

through, His right Arm is o'er us, His right . . .

. . us, will guide . . . . us through, He will guide, . .

right . . . Arm is .. o'er .. us, ... He will

right Arm is o'er us, His right . . . Arm .. is .. o'er us, is

Arm, . . . is o'er us, His right . . . Arm . . . is o'er us, His

guide . . . . us, will guide . . . . .

guide . . . . us, He will guide . . . .

o'er us, His right . . . Arm is o'er us, His right

48

W
guide . . . . us through,
guide . . . . us through, His right
through, He'll guide us through, His right Arm is o'er us, His
guide . . . . us through, His right Arm is o'er us, His right . .
8va
His right Arm is o'er us, His right . .
Arm is o'er us. His right . . Arm is o'er . . .
right . . . . Arm, His right Arm is o'er us,
. . . . Arm, His right . . . Arm is o'er . . .
Arm is o'er us, is o'er us, is o'er . . us,
. . . . . . us, is o'er us, is o'er . . us,
is . . o'er . . us, is o'er . . us,
us, is . . . o'er . . us,

X SOLO.

Christ . . hath gone be - fore . . . us,

Christ . . hath gone be - fore . . . us: Chris - tians,

Chris - tians, fol - - - - low . . you,

Y Vivace. ♩ = 134.

Vivace. ♩ = 138.

colla voce.

CHORUS.

Chris - tians, fol - low you, fol - - low

Chris - tians, fol - low you, fol - - low

Chris - tians, fol - low you, fol - low

Chris - tians, fol - low you, fol - low

8284.

rall.
you, Chris - tians, fol - low
you, Chris - tians, fol - low
you, Chris - tians, fol - low
you, Chris - tians, fol - low
8va
rall.
Adagio. ♩ = 56. ff Solo col Coro.
you, Chris - tians, fol - low
ff
you, Chris - tians, fol - low, fol - low
ff
you, Chris - tians, fol - low
ff
you, Chris - tians, fol - low
Adagio. ♩ = 56.
8va
ff
you!
you!
you!
you!

THE END

NOVELLO'S ORIGINAL OCTAVO EDITIONS
OF
Oratorios, Cantatas, Odes, Masses, &c.

FRANZ ABT.

THE FAYS' FROLIC (Female voices) ...	2/6	—	—
SPRINGTIME (ditto) (Sol-fa, 0/6)	2/6	—	—
SUMMER (ditto) ...	2/6	—	—
THE GOLDEN CITY (ditto) (Sol-fa, 0/6)	2/6	—	—
THE WISHING STONE (ditto) ...	2/6	—	—
THE WATER FAIRIES (ditto) ...	2/6	—	—
THE SILVER CLOUD (ditto) ...	2/6	—	—
MINSTER BELLS (ditto) ...	2/6	—	—

J. H. ADAMS.

A DAY IN SUMMER (Sol-fa, 0/6) ...	1/6	—	—

T. ADAMS.

THE CROSS OF CHRIST (Sol-fa, 0/6)	1/0	—	—
THE HOLY CHILD (Sol-fa, 8/6)	1/0	—	—
THE RAINBOW OF PEACE ...	1/0	—	—

B. AGUTTER.

MISSA DE SANCTO ALBANO (English) ...	3/0	4/0	5/0
MISSA DE BEATA MARIÂ VIRGINE, IN C (English) (Female voices) ...	2/6		

THOMAS ANDERTON.

YULE TIDE ...	1/6	2/0	3/0
THE NORMAN BARON ...	1/0	—	—
WRECK OF THE HESPERUS (Sol-fa, 0/4)	1/0	—	—

J. H. ANGER.

A SONG OF THANKSGIVING.. ...	1/6	—	—

W. I. ARGENT.

MASS, IN B FLAT ...	2/6	—	—

P. ARMES.

HEZEKIAH	2/6		
ST. JOHN THE EVANGELIST	2/6		
ST. BARNABAS	2/0		

A. D. ARNOTT.

YOUNG LOCHINVAR (Sol-fa, 0/6)	2/6	—	—
THE BALLAD OF CARMILHAN (Sol-fa, 1/6)	2/6	—	—

E. ASPA.

THE GIPSIES	1/0		
ENDYMION ...	4/0		

ASTORGA.

STABAT MATER ...	1/0	1/6	

BACH.

MASS, IN B MINOR	2/6	3/0	4/0
MISSA BREVIS, IN A	1/6		
THE PASSION (S. Matthew)	2/6	3/0	
Abridged, as used at St. Paul's			
THE PASSION (S. John)	2/0	3/6	4/0
CHRISTMAS ORATORIO	3/0	3/6	4/0
(Parts 3 & 4)	1/6		
MAGNIFICAT	1/0		
GOD GOETH UP WITH SHOUTING	1/0		
GOD SO LOVED THE WORLD	1/0		
GOD'S TIME IS THE BEST (Sol-fa, 0/6) ...	1/0		
MY SPIRIT WAS IN HEAVINESS	1/0		
O LIGHT EVERLASTING	1/0		
BIDE WITH US	1/0		
A STRONGHOLD SURE (Choruses only) (Sol-fa, 0/6)	1/0		
BE NOT AFRAID (Sol-fa, 0/6)	0/8		
BLESSING, GLORY, AND WISDOM	0/8		
I WRESTLE AND PRAY (Sol-fa, 0/2)	0/4		
THOU GUIDE OF ISRAEL	1/0		
JESU, PRICELESS TREASURE	1/0		
WHEN WILL GOD RECALL MY SPIRIT	1/0		
JESUS, NOW WILL WE PRAISE THEE	1/0		

A. S. BAKER.

COMMUNION SERVICE, IN E ...	1/6	—	—

J. BARNBY.

REBEKAH (Sol-fa, 0/8)	1/0	1/6	2/6
THE LORD IS KING (97th Psalm) (Sol-fa, 1/0)	1/6	2/0	—

LEONARD BARNES.

THE BRIDAL DAY	2/6	—	—

J. F. BARNETT.

THE ANCIENT MARINER (Sol-fa, 2/0) ...	2/6	4/0	5/0
THE RAISING OF LAZARUS ...	6/0	—	9/0
PARADISE AND THE PERI ...	4/0	—	—
THE WISHING BELL (Female voices)(Sol-fa, 1/-)	2/6	—	—

BEETHOVEN.

THE PRAISE OF MUSIC ...	1/6	2/0	3/0
RUINS OF ATHENS	1/0	1/6	2/6
ENGEDI; OR, DAVID IN THE WILDERNESS	1/0	1/6	2/6
MOUNT OF OLIVES (Choruses, Sol-fa, 0/8)	1/0	1/6	2/6
MASS, IN C ...	1/0	1/6	2/6
COMMUNION SERVICE, IN C ...	1/0	—	3/0
MASS, IN D ...	2/0	2/6	4/0
THE CHORAL SYMPHONY ...	2/6	—	—
Ditto, VOCAL PART (Sol-fa, 0/6)	1/0		
THE CHORAL FANTASIA (Sol-fa, 0/3) ...	1/0	—	—
A CALM SEA AND A PROSPEROUS VOYAGE	0/4	—	—
MEEK, AS THOU LIVEDST ...	0/3	—	—

KAREL BENDL.

WATER-SPRITE'S REVENGE (Female voices) ...	1/0	—	—

WILFRED BENDALL.

THE LADY OF SHALOTT (Female vv.)(Sol-fa, 1/0)	2/6	—	—
A LEGEND OF BREGENZ ...	1/6	—	—

SIR JULIUS BENEDICT.

ST. PETER	3/0	3/6	5/0
THE LEGEND OF ST. CECILIA (Sol-fa, 1/6)	2/6	3/0	4/0
PASSION MUSIC FROM ST. PETER ...	1/6	—	—

GEORGE J. BENNETT.

EASTER HYMN ...	1/0	—	—

SIR W. STERNDALE BENNETT.

THE MAY QUEEN (Sol-fa, 1/0)	2/6	3/6	2/6
THE WOMAN OF SAMARIA (Sol-fa, 1/0)...	4/0	—	6/0
INTERNATIONAL EXHIBITION ODE (1862)	1/0	—	—

G. R. BETJEMANN.

THE SONG OF THE WESTERN MEN ...	1/0		

W. R. BEXFIELD.

ISRAEL RESTORED ...	4/0	—	6/0

HUGH BLAIR.

HARVEST-TIDE	1/0	—	—
BLESSED ARE THEY WHO WATCH (Advent)	1/6	—	—

JOSIAH BOOTH.

THE DAY OF REST (Female voices) (Sol-fa, 1/0) ...	2/6		

E. M. BOYCE.

THE LAY OF THE BROWN ROSARY ...	1/6		
YOUNG LOCHINVAR ...	1/6		
THE SANDS OF CORRIEMIE (Female voices)	1/6		

J. BRADFORD.

HARVEST CANTATA	1/6		
THE SONG OF JUBILEE	1/6		

W. F. BRADSHAW.

GASPAR BECERRA ...	1/6		

J. BRAHMS.

A SONG OF DESTINY ...	1/0	—	—

C. BRAUN.

SIGURD ...	5/0	—	—

J. C. BRIDGE.

DANIEL	2/6		
RESURGAM	2/6		
RUDEL	4/0		

J. F. BRIDGE.

BOADICEA	2/6		
CALLIRHOE (Sol-fa, 1/6)...	2/6	3/0	4/0
HYMN TO THE CREATOR	2/0		
MOUNT MORIAH	2/0		
NINEVEH	2/6	4/0	6/0
ROCK OF AGES (Latin and English) (Sol-fa, 0/4)...	1/0		
THE CRADLE OF CHRIST ("Stabat Mater Speciosa")	1/6		
THE FLAG OF ENGLAND (Sol-fa, 0/9)	1/6	—	—
THE INCHCAPE ROCK ...	1/0	—	—
THE LORD'S PRAYER (Sol-fa, 0/6)	1/0	—	—

1/9/97.

DUDLEY BUCK.
THE LIGHT OF ASIA	3/0	3/6	5/0

EDWARD BUNNETT.
OUT OF THE DEEP (130th Psalm)	1/0	—	—

W. BYRD.
MASS FOR FOUR VOICES (in F minor)	2/6	—	—

CARISSIMI
JEPHTHAH	1/0	—	—

F. D. CARNELL.
SUPPLICATION	5/0	—	—

GEORGE CARTER.
SINFONIA CANTATA (116th Psalm)	2/0	—	2/6

WILLIAM CARTER.
PLACIDA	2/0	2/6	4/0

CHERUBINI.
REQUIEM MASS, C MINOR (Latin and English)	1/0	1/6	2/6
SECOND MASS, IN D MINOR	2/0	2/6	2/6
THIRD MASS (Coronation)	1/0	1/6	2/6
FOURTH MASS, IN C	1/0	1/6	2/6

E. T. CHIPP.
JOB	4/0	—	—
NAOMI	3/0	—	—

HAMILTON CLARKE.
PEPIN THE PIPPIN (Operetta), both Notations	2/6		
(Ditto, Sol-fa, 0 9)			
THE MISSING DUKE (Operetta) (Sol-fa, 0/9)	2/6	—	
THE DAISY CHAIN (Operetta) (Sol-fa, 0,9)	2/6	—	
DRUMS AND VOICES (Operetta) (Sol-fa, 0,9)	2/6	—	
HORNPIPE HARRY (Sol-fa, 0;9)	2/6	—	

FREDERICK CORDER.
THE BRIDAL OF TRIERMAIN (Sol-fa, 1/0)	2/6	—	—

SIR MICHAEL COSTA.
THE DREAM	1/6	—	—

H. COWARD.
THE STORY OF BETHANY (Sol-fa, 1/6)	2/6	3/0	

F. H. COWEN.
ST. JOHN'S EVE (Sol-fa, 1/6)	2/6	3/0	4/0
A SONG OF THANKSGIVING	1/6	—	—
SLEEPING BEAUTY (Sol-fa, 1/6)	3/0	3/0	4/0
RUTH (Sol-fa, 1/6)	2/0	2/6	5/0
SUMMER ON THE RIVER (Female vv.) (Sol-fa, 0/9)	2/0	—	
THE WATER LILY	2/0	—	
VILLAGE SCENES (Female voices) (Sol-fa, 0/9)	1/6	—	
CHRISTMAS SCENES (Female voices) (Sol-fa, 0/9)	2/0	—	
THE ROSE OF LIFE (Female voices) (Sol-fa, 0/9)	2/0	—	
A DAUGHTER OF THE SEA (Female voices)	2/0	—	
(Ditto Sol-fa, 1/0)			
DREAM OF ENDYMION	2/6	—	

J. MAUDE CRAMENT.
I WILL MAGNIFY THEE, O GOD (145th Psalm)	2/6	—	
LITTLE RED RIDING-HOOD (Female voices)	3/0	—	

W. CRESER.
EUDORA (A dramatic Idyll)	2/6	—	

W. CROTCH.
PALESTINE	2/0	3/6	5/0

W. H. CUMMINGS.
THE FAIRY RING	2/6	—	

W. G. CUSINS.
TE DEUM	1/6	—	

FÉLICIEN DAVID.
THE DESERT (Male voices)	1/6	2/0	—

H. WALFORD DAVIES.
HERVÉ RIEL	1/0	—	

P. H. DIEMER.
BETHANY	4/0	—	

M. E. DOORLY.
LAZARUS	2/6	—	

F. G. DOSSERT.
MASS, IN E MINOR	4/0	—	—
COMMUNION SERVICE, IN E MINOR	2/0	—	—

LUCY K. DOWNING.
A PARABLE IN SONG	2/0	—	—

F. DUNKLEY.
THE WRECK OF THE HESPERUS	1/6	—	—

ANTONIN DVOŘÁK.
ST. LUDMILA	5/0	6/0	7/6
Ditto (German and Bohemian Words)	4/0		
THE SPECTRE'S BRIDE (Sol-fa, 1/6)	3/6	7/6	6/0
Ditto (German and Bohemian Words)	4/0		
STABAT MATER	3/6	3/0	4/0
PATRIOTIC HYMN	1/6	—	—
Ditto (German and Bohemian Words)	2/0	—	
REQUIEM MASS	5/0	6/0	7/6
MASS, IN D	2/6	—	
COMMUNION SERVICE, IN D	2/6	—	

A. E. DYER.
SALVATOR MUNDI	2/6	—	
ELECTRA OF SOPHOCLES	1/6	2/0	

H. J. EDWARDS.
THE ASCENSION	2/6	—	
THE EPIPHANY	2/0	—	
PRAISE TO THE HOLIEST	1/6	—	

EDWARD ELGAR.
THE BLACK KNIGHT	2/0	—	
THE LIGHT OF LIFE (Lux Christi)	2/6	—	
KING OLAF (Sol-fa, Choruses only, 1/6)	2/0	—	
THE BANNER OF ST. GEORGE (Sol-fa, 1/0)	1/6	—	
TE DEUM AND BENEDICTUS	1/0	—	

ROSALIND F. ELLICOTT.
ELYSIUM	1/0	—	
THE BIRTH OF SONG	1/6	—	

GUSTAV ERNEST.
ALL THE YEAR ROUND (Female vv.) (Sol-fa, 0/9)	2/0	—	

T. FACER.
RED RIDING-HOOD'S RECEPTION (Operetta)	2/6	—	
(Ditto, Sol-fa, 0/6)			

E. FANING.
BUTTERCUPS AND DAISIES (Female voices)	2/6	—	
(Ditto, Sol-fa, 0/6)			

HENRY FARMER.
MASS, IN B FLAT (Latin and English) (Sol-fa, 1/0)	2/0	2/6	2/6

MYLES B. FOSTER.
THE LADY OF THE ISLES	1/6	—	
THE ANGELS OF THE BELLS (Female voices)	1/6	—	
(Ditto, Sol-fa, 0/6)			
THE BONNIE FISHWIVES (Female vv.) (Sol-fa, 0/9)	2/6	—	
SNOW FAIRIES (Female voices)	1/6	—	
THE COMING OF THE KING (Female voices)	1/6	—	
(Ditto, Sol-fa, 0,8)			

ROBERT FRANZ.
PRAISE YE THE LORD (117th Psalm)	1/0	—	

NIELS W. GADE.
PSYCHE (Sol-fa, 1,6)	2/6	3/0	4/0
SPRING'S MESSAGE (Sol-fa, 0 3)	0/6	—	
ERL-KING'S DAUGHTER (Sol-fa, 0/8)	1/0	1/6	4/0
ZION	1/0	1/6	4/0
THE CRUSADERS (Sol-fa, 1.0)	2/0	2/6	4/0
COMALA	2/0	2/6	4/0
CHRISTMAS EVE (Sol-fa, 0 4)	1/0	1/6	—

HENRY GADSBY.
LORD OF THE ISLES (Sol-fa, 1/6)	2/6	—	
ALCESTIS (Male voices)	4/0	—	
COLUMBUS (Male voices)	2/6	—	

F. W. GALPIN.
YE OLDE ENGLYSHE PASTYMES	1/6	—	

G. GARRETT.
HARVEST CANTATA (Sol-fa, 0/6)	1/0	—	
THE SHUNAMMITE	3/0	—	
THE TWO ADVENTS	1/6	—	

R. MACHILL GARTH.
EZEKIEL	4/0	4/6	—
THE WILD HUNTSMAN	1/6	1/6	—

A. R. GAUL.

AROUND THE WINTER FIRE (Female voices)	2/6	—	—
(DITTO, SOL-FA, 0/9)			
A SONG OF LIFE (Ode to Music) (SOL-FA, 0/6)	1/0	—	—
JOAN OF ARC (SOL-FA, 1/0)	2/6	3/0	4/0
PASSION SERVICE	2/6	3/0	4/0
RUTH (SOL-FA, 0/9)	2/0	3/6	4/0
THE HOLY CITY (SOL-FA, 1/0)	2/0	3/0	4/0
THE TEN VIRGINS (SOL-FA, 1/0)	2/6	3/0	4/0
ISRAEL IN THE WILDERNESS (SOL-FA, 1/0)	2/6	3/0	4/0
TOILERS OF THE DEEP (Female voices)	2/0	—	—
UNA	2/6	3/0	4/0
(DITTO, SOL-FA, 1/0)			
THE LEGEND OF THE WOOD (Female voices)	1/0	—	—
(DITTO, SOL-FA, 0/8)			
TOILERS OF THE DEEP (Female voices)	2/0	—	—

FR. GERNSHEIM.

SALAMIS. A TRIUMPH SONG (Male voices)	1/6	—	—

E. OUSELEY GILBERT.

SANTA CLAUS AND HIS COMRADES (Operetta)	2/0	—	—
(DITTO, SOL-FA, 0/8)			

F. E. GLADSTONE.

PHILIPPI	2/6	—	—

GLUCK.

ORPHEUS (CHORUSES, SOL-FA, 1/0)	2/6	—	—

HERMANN GOETZ.

BY THE WATERS OF BABYLON (137th Psalm)	1/0	—	—
NŒNIA	1/0	—	—
THE WATER-LILY (Male voices)	1/6	—	—

A. M. GOODHART.

EARL HALDAN'S DAUGHTER	1/0	—	—
ARETHUSA	2/0	—	—
SIR ANDREW BARTON	1/0	—	—

CH. GOUNOD.

MORS ET VITA (Latin or English)	3/0	4/6	7/6
DITTO, SOL-FA (Latin and English)	2/0	—	—
REQUIEM MASS, from "Mors et Vita"	2/0	6/0	7/6
THE REDEMPTION (English Words) (SOL-FA, 2/0)	3/0	4/0	7/6
DITTO (French Words)	3/6	—	—
DITTO (German Words)	10/6	—	—
MESSE SOLENNELLE (ST. CECILIA)	1/0	1/6	2/6
OUT OF DARKNESS	1/0	—	—
COMMUNION SERVICE (Messe Solennelle)	1/6	2/0	3/0
DITTO (Troisième Messe Solennelle)	2/6	—	—
TROISIÈME MESSE SOLENNELLE	2/6	—	—
DE PROFUNDIS (130th Psalm) (Latin Words)	1/0	—	—
DITTO (Out of darkness)	1/0	—	—
THE SEVEN WORDS OF OUR SAVIOUR ON THE CROSS (Filiæ Jerusalem)	1/0	—	—
DAUGHTERS OF JERUSALEM	1/6	—	—
GALLIA (SOL-FA, 0/4)	1/0	—	—

C. H. GRAUN.

THE PASSION OF OUR LORD (Der Tod Jesu)	2/0	3/6	4/0
TE DEUM	2/0	3/6	4/0

ALAN GRAY.

THE WIDOW OF ZAREPHATH	2/0	—	—
ARETHUSA	1/6	—	—
THE LEGEND OF THE ROCK-BUOY BELL	1/6	—	—

J. O. GRIMM.

THE SOUL'S ASPIRATION	1/0	—	—

G. HALFORD.

THE PARACLETE	2/0	—	—

E. V. HALL.

IS IT NOTHING TO YOU (SOL-FA, 0/3)	0/6	—	—

HANDEL.

ALEXANDER'S FEAST	2/0	3/6	4/0
ACIS AND GALATEA	1/0	1/6	2/6
DITTO, New Edition, edited by J. Barnby (SOL-FA, 1/0)	1/0	1/6	2/6
ALCESTE	2/0	—	—
SEMELE	2/0	—	—
THE PASSION	2/0	—	—
THE TRIUMPH OF TIME AND TRUTH	2/0	3/0	4/0
ALEXANDER BALUS	2/0	—	—
HERCULES	2/0	—	—
ATHALIAH	2/0	—	—
ESTHER	2/0	3/0	4/0
SUSANNA	2/0	3/0	4/0
THEODORA	2/0	3/0	4/0
BELSHAZZAR	2/0	3/0	4/0
THE MESSIAH, edited by V. Novello (SOL-FA, 1/0)	2/0	3/0	4/0
THE MESSIAH, ditto, Pocket Edition	1/0	1/6	2/0
THE MESSIAH, edited by W. T. Best	2/0	3/0	4/0
ISRAEL IN EGYPT, edited by Mendelssohn	2/0	3/0	4/0
ISRAEL IN EGYPT, edited by V. Novello, Pocket Edit.	1/0	1/6	2/0
JUDAS MACCABÆUS (SOL-FA, 1/0)	2/0	3/0	4/0
JUDAS MACCABÆUS, Pocket Edition	1/0	1/6	2/0

HANDEL.—Continued.

SAMSON (SOL-FA, 1/0)	2/0	3/6	4/0
SOLOMON	2/0	3/6	4/0
JEPHTHA	2/0	3/6	4/0
JOSHUA	2/0	3/6	4/0
DEBORAH	2/0	3/6	4/0
SAUL	2/0	3/6	4/0
CHANDOS TE DEUM	1/0	1/6	2/0
DETTINGEN TE DEUM	1/0	1/6	2/6
UTRECHT JUBILATE	1/0	—	—
O COME, LET US SING UNTO THE LORD (5th Chandos Anthem)	1/6	—	—
O PRAISE THE LORD (6th Chandos Anthem)	1/0	—	—
CORONATION AND FUNERAL ANTHEMS	—	—	5/0
Or, singly:—			
THE KING SHALL REJOICE	0/6		
ZADOK THE PRIEST	0/6		
MY HEART IS INDITING	0/6		
LET THY HAND BE STRENGTHENED	0/6		
THE WAYS OF ZION	1/0		
ODE ON ST. CECILIA'S DAY	1/0	1/6	2/6
L'ALLEGRO	2/0	3/6	4/0
DIXIT DOMINUS (from Psalm cx.)	1/0	—	—

F. K. HATTERSLEY.

ROBERT OF SICILY	2/6	—	—

HAYDN.

THE CREATION (SOL-FA, 1/0)	2/0	3/6	4/0
THE CREATION, Pocket Edition	1/0	1/6	2/0
THE SEASONS	2/0	3/6	4/0
Each Season, singly (SPRING, Tonic Sol-fa, 6d.)	1/0		
FIRST MASS, IN B FLAT (Latin)	1/0	1/6	2/6
DITTO (Latin and English)	1/0	1/6	2/6
SECOND MASS, IN C (Latin)	1/0	1/6	2/6
THIRD MASS (IMPERIAL) (Latin and English)	1/0	1/6	2/6
DITTO (Latin)	1/0	1/6	2/6
SIXTEENTH MASS (Latin)	1/0	3/0	3/0
THE PASSION; OR, SEVEN LAST WORDS OF OUR SAVIOUR ON THE CROSS	2/0	3/6	4/0
TE DEUM (English and Latin)	1/0	—	—
INSANÆ ET VANÆ CURÆ (Ditto)	0/4	—	—

BATTISON HAYNES.

THE FAIRIES' ISLE (Female voices)	2/6	—	—
A SEA DREAM (Female voices) (SOL-FA, 0/6)	2/0	—	—

H. HEALE.

JUBILEE ODE	1/0	—	—

C. SWINNERTON HEAP.

FAIR ROSAMOND (SOL-FA, 2/0)	2/6	4/0	5/0

EDWARD HECHT.

ERIC THE DANE	2/0	—	—
O MAY I JOIN THE CHOIR INVISIBLE	1/0	—	—

GEORGE HENSCHEL.

OUT OF DARKNESS (130th Psalm)	2/0	—	—
TE DEUM LAUDAMUS, IN C	1/6	—	—
STABAT MATER	2/6	—	—

HENRY HILES.

THE CRUSADERS	2/6	—	—

FERDINAND HILLER.

NALA AND DAMAYANTI	4/0	—	—
A SONG OF VICTORY (SOL-FA, 0/9)	1/0	1/6	—

H. E. HODSON.

THE GOLDEN LEGEND	2/0	—	—

HEINRICH HOFMANN.

FAIR MELUSINA	2/0	3/6	4/0
CINDERELLA	4/6	—	—
SONG OF THE NORNS (Female voices)	1/0	—	—

C. HOLLAND.

AFTER THE SKIRMISH	1/0	—	—

HUMMEL.

FIRST MASS, IN B FLAT	1/0	1/6	2/6
COMMUNION SERVICE, ditto	2/0	—	—
SECOND MASS, IN E FLAT	1/0	1/6	2/6
COMMUNION SERVICE, ditto	2/0	—	—
THIRD MASS, IN D	2/0	—	—
COMMUNION SERVICE, ditto	2/0	1/6	2/6
ALMA VIRGO (Latin and English)	0/4	—	—
QUOD IN ORBE (Ditto)	0/4	—	—

W. H. HUNT.

STABAT MATER	2/0	4/6	—

G. F. HUNTLEY.

VICTORIA; OR, THE BARD'S PROPHECY	2/0	—	—
(DITTO, SOL-FA, 1/0)			

H. H. HUSS.

AVE MARIA (Female voices) ... ... 1/0 — —

F. ILIFFE.

SWEET ECHO ... ... 1/0 — —

W. JACKSON.

THE YEAR ... ... 2/0 2/6 —

D. JENKINS.

DAVID AND SAUL (Sol-fa, 2/0) ... ... 2/0 3/6 —

A. JENSEN.

THE FEAST OF ADONIS ... ... 1/0 — —

W. JOHNSON.

ECCE HOMO ... ... 2/0 — —

C. WARWICK JORDAN.

BLOW YE THE TRUMPET IN ZION ... ... 1/6 — —

N. KILBURN.

THE SILVER STAR (Female voices) ... ... 1/0 — —
THE LORD IS MY SHEPHERD (23rd Psalm) ... 0/6 — —
BY THE WATERS OF BABYLON ... ... 1/0 — —

ALFRED KING.

THE EPIPHANY ... ... 2/0 — —

OLIVER KING.

BY THE WATERS OF BABYLON (137th Psalm)... 1/6 — —
THE NAIADS (Female voices) ... ... 2/6 — —
THE SANDS O' DEE ... ... 1/0 — —
THE ROMANCE OF THE ROSES ... ... 2/6 — —

J. KINROSS.

SONGS IN A VINEYARD (Female vv.) (Sol-fa, 0/6) 2/6 — —

H. LAHEE.

THE SLEEPING BEAUTY (Female vv.)(Sol-fa, 0/6) 2/6 — —

LEONARDO LEO.

DIXIT DOMINUS ... ... 1/0 1/6 —

H. LESLIE.

THE FIRST CHRISTMAS MORN ... ... 2/6 — —

F. LISZT.

THE LEGEND OF ST. ELIZABETH 3/0 3/6 6/0
THIRTEENTH PSALM ... ... 2/0 — —

C. H. LLOYD.

ALCESTIS (Sol-fa, 1/6) ... ... 2/0 — —
ANDROMEDA 2/0 3/6 5/0
HERO AND LEANDER ... ... 1/6 — —
THE SONG OF BALDER ... ... 1/0 — —
THE LONGBEARDS' SAGA (Male voices) ... 1/6 — —
THE GLEANERS' HARVEST (Female voices) 2/6 — —
A SONG OF JUDGMENT 2/6 3/0 6/0
ROSSALL ... ... 2/0 — —
SIR OGIE AND THE LADIE ELSIE ... ... 1/6 — —

CLEMENT LOCKNANE.

THE ELFIN QUEEN (Female voices) ... ... 2/6 — —

W. H. LONGHURST.

THE VILLAGE FAIR ... ... 2/0 2/6 —

HAMISH MacCUNN.

LAY OF THE LAST MINSTREL (Sol-fa, 1/6) 2/6 3/0 6/0
LORD ULLIN'S DAUGHTER (Sol-fa, 0/6)... 1/0 — —

G. A. MACFARREN.

SONGS IN A CORNFIELD (Female voices) ... 1/6 — —
(Ditto, Sol-fa, 0/9)
MAY-DAY 1/0 1/6 2/6
THE SOLDIER'S LEGACY (Operetta) ... 6/0 — —
OUTWARD BOUND ... ... 1/0 — 2/6

A. C. MACKENZIE.

THE DREAM OF JUBAL 2/6 3/0 6/0
(Ditto, Choruses only, Sol-fa, 1/0)
THE STORY OF SAYID 2/0 3/6 6/0
JASON 2/6 3/0 6/0
THE BRIDE (Sol-fa, 0/8)... ... ... 1/0 — —
THE ROSE OF SHARON (Sol-fa, 2/0) ... 6/0 6/0 7/6
JUBILEE ODE (Sol-fa, 1/6) ... ... 2/6 — —
THE COTTER'S SATURDAY NIGHT (Sol-fa, 1/0) 2/0 — —
THE NEW COVENANT ... ... 3/0 — —
VENI, CREATOR SPIRITUS ... ... 2/0 — —
BETHLEHEM 2/0 6/0 7/6
Ditto, Act II., separately ... ... 2/6 — —

G. C. MARTIN.

TE DEUM AND ANTIPHON ... ... 0/6 — —

J. B. McEWEN.

THE VISION OF JACOB ... ... 2/0 — —

C. MACPHERSON.

BY THE WATERS OF BABYLON (137th Psalm) ... 2/0 — —

L. MANCINELLI.

ERO E LEANDRO ... ... 4/0 — —

F. W. MARKULL.

ROLAND'S HORN (Male voices) ... ... 2/0 — —

F. E. MARSHALL.

PRINCE SPRITE (Female voices) ... ... 2/6 — —

J. T. MASSER.

HARVEST CANTATA ... ... 1/0 — —

J. H. MEE.

HORATIUS (Male voices) ... ... 1/0 — —
DELPHI, A LEGEND OF HELLAS (Male voices) 1/0 — —

MENDELSSOHN.

ELIJAH (Sol-fa, 1/0) 2/0 2/6 4/0
ELIJAH (Pocket Edition) 1/0 1/6 2/0
AS THE HART PANTS (42nd Psalm) (Sol-fa, 0/6) 1/0 — —
COME, LET US SING (95th Psalm) ... 1/0 —
WHEN ISRAEL OUT OF EGYPT CAME ... 1/0 } — 3/0
(Ditto, Sol-fa, 0/9)
NOT UNTO US, O LORD (115th Psalm) ... 1/0 — —
ST. PAUL (Sol-fa, 1/0) 2/0 2/6 4/0
ST. PAUL (Pocket Edition) 1/0 1/6 2/0
HYMN OF PRAISE (Lobgesang) (Sol-fa, 1/0) 1/0 1/6 2/6
LORD, HOW LONG WILT THOU (Sol-fa, 0/4) ... 1/0 — —
HEAR MY PRAYER (s. solo and chorus) (Sol-fa, 0/2) 1/0 — —
Ditto   Ditto 0/4 — —
LAUDA SION (Praise Jehovah) (Sol-fa, 0/9) 2/0 2/6 5/0
THE FIRST WALPURGIS NIGHT (Sol-fa, 1/0)... 1/0 1/6 3/0
MIDSUMMER NIGHT'S DREAM (Female voices) 1/0 — —
ATHALIE (Sol-fa, 1/0) 2/0 2/6 4/0
ANTIGONE (Male voices) (Sol-fa, 1/0) ... 1/0 — —
MAN IS MORTAL (8 voices) ... ... 1/0 — —
FESTGESANG (Hymns of Praise) ... ... 1/0 — —
Ditto   (Male voices) ... ... 1/0 — —
CHRISTUS (Sol-fa, 0/6) ... ... 1/0 — —
THREE MOTETS FOR FEMALE VOICES ... 1/0 — —
SON AND STRANGER (Operetta) ... ... 1/0 — —
LORELEY (Sol-fa, 0/6) ... ... 1/0 — —
ŒDIPUS AT COLONOS (Male voices) ... 1/0 — —
TO THE SONS OF ART   (Ditto)   (Sol-fa, 0/3) 1/0 — —
JUDGE ME, O GOD (43rd Psalm) (Sol-fa, 0/1½) 0/4 — —
WHY RAGE FIERCELY THE HEATHEN ... 0/4 — —
MY GOD, WHY, O WHY HAST THOU FOR-
   SAKEN ME (22nd Psalm) ... ... 0/6 — —
SING TO THE LORD (98th Psalm) ... 0/6 — —
SIX ANTHEMS for the Cathedral at Berlin. For
   8 voices, arranged in 4 parts ... ... 0/6 — —
AVE MARIA (Saviour of Sinners), 8 voices ... 1/0 — —

R. D. METCALFE and A. KENNEDY.

PRINCE FERDINAND (Operetta) (Sol-fa, 0/9) ... 2/0 — —

MEYERBEER.

NINETY-FIRST PSALM (Latin) ... ... 1/0 — —
   Ditto   (English) ... ... 1/0 — —

A. MOFFAT.

A CHRISTMAS DREAM (A Cantata for Children) ... 1/6 — —
(Ditto, Sol-fa, 0/4)

B. MOLIQUE.

ABRAHAM 3/0 3/6 5/0

MOZART.

KING THAMOS ... ... 1/0 1/6 —
FIRST MASS (Latin and English) 1/0 1/6 2/6
SEVENTH MASS, IN B FLAT ... ... 1/0 — —
COMMUNION SERVICE, IN B FLAT, ditto ... 1/6 — —
TWELFTH MASS (Latin) 1/0 1/6 2/6
   Ditto   (Latin and English) (Sol-fa, 0/9) 1/0 1/6 2/6
REQUIEM MASS 1/0 1/6 2/6
   Ditto   (Latin and English) (Sol-fa, 1/0)... 1/0 1/6 2/6
LITANIA DE VENERABILI ALTARIS (E♭) ... 1/6 — —
LITANIA DE VENERABILI SACRAMENTO (B♭) 1/6 4/0 6/0
SPLENDENTE TE, DEUS   First Motet 0/3 — —
O GOD, WHEN THOU APPEAREST   ditto 0/3 — —
HAVE MERCY, O LORD ...   Second Motet 0/3 — —
GLORY, HONOUR, PRAISE   Third Motet 0/3 — —

E. MUNDELLA.

VICTORY OF SONG (Female voices) ... ... 1/0 — —

DR. JOHN NAYLOR.

JEREMIAH ... ... 3/0 — —

JOSEF NEŠVERA.

DE PROFUNDIS ... ... 2/6 — —

NOVELLO'S OCTAVO EDITION OF ORATORIOS, &c.—*Continued.*

E. A. NUNN.

MASS, IN C ... ... **2/0** — —

REV. SIR FREDK. OUSELEY.

THE MARTYRDOM OF ST. POLYCARP ... ... **2/6** — —

R. P. PAINE.

THE LORD REIGNETH (93rd Psalm) ... ... **1/0** — —

PALESTRINA.

MISSA ASSUMPTA EST MARIA ... ... **2/6** — —
MISSA PAPÆ MARCELLI ... ... **2/0** — —
MISSA BREVIS ... ... **2/6** — —
MISSA "O ADMIRABILE COMMERCIUM" ... **2/6** — —

H. W. PARKER.

THE KOBOLDS ... ... **1/0** — —
HORA NOVISSIMA ... ... **3/6** — —

C. H. H. PARRY.

DE PROFUNDIS (130th Psalm) ... ... **2/0** — —
ODE ON ST. CECILIA'S DAY (Sol-fa, 1/0) ... **2/0** — —
BLEST PAIR OF SIRENS (Sol-fa, 0/8) ... **1/0** — —
THE GLORIES OF OUR BLOOD AND STATE **1/0** — —
PROMETHEUS UNBOUND ... ... **3/0** — —
JUDITH (Choruses, Sol-fa, 2/0)... ... ... **6/0** 6/0 7/6
L'ALLEGRO (Sol-fa, 1/6) ... ... **3/0** — —
ETON ... ... **3/0** — —
THE LOTUS-EATERS (The Choric Song) ... **3/0** — —
JOB (Choruses, Sol-fa, 1/0) ... ... **2/6** — —
KING SAUL **6/0** 8/0 7/6
INVOCATION TO MUSIC ... ... **2/6** — —
MAGNIFICAT ... ... **1/6** — —

DR. JOSEPH PARRY.

NEBUCHADNEZZAR **3/0** 6/0 5/0
  Ditto,   (Sol-fa) **1/6** 2/0 3/6

B. PARSONS.

THE CRUSADER ... ... **2/0** — —

T. M. PATTISON.

MAY DAY ... ... **1/6** — —
THE MIRACLES OF CHRIST (Sol-fa, 0/9) ... **2/0** — —
THE ANCIENT MARINER ... ... **2/6** — —
THE LAY OF THE LAST MINSTREL ... ... **2/6** — —

A. L. PEACE.

ST. JOHN THE BAPTIST ... ... **2/6** — —

A. H. D. PRENDERGAST.

THE SECOND ADVENT... ... ... **1/6** — —

PERGOLESI.

STABAT MATER (Female voices) (Sol-fa, 0/6) ... **1/0** — —

CIRO PINSUTI.

PHANTOMS—FANTÂSMI NELL' OMBRA ... **1/0** — —

E. PROUT.

DAMON AND PHINTIAS (Male voices) ... **2/6** — —
THE RED CROSS KNIGHT (Sol-fa, 2,0) ... **4/0** 4/6 6/0
THE HUNDREDTH PSALM ... ... **1/9** — —
FREEDOM ... ... **1/0** — —
HEREWARD ... ... **4/0** — —
QUEEN AIMÉE (Female voices) ... ... **2/6** — —

PURCELL.

DIDO AND ÆNEAS ... ... **2/6** — —
TE DEUM AND JUBILATE, IN D ... ... **1/0** — —
  Ditto   (Edited by Dr. Bridge) (Sol-fa, 0/6) ... **1/0** — —
ODE ON ST. CECILIA'S DAY ... ... **2/0** — —
THREE SCENES, from "King Arthur" ... ... **1/6** — —

LADY RAMSAY.

THE BLESSED DAMOZEL ... ... **2/6** — —

F. J. READ.

THE SONG OF HANNAH ... ... **1/0** — —

J. F. H. READ.

HAROLD ... ... **4/0** — 6/0
BARTIMEUS ... ... **1/6** — —
CARACTACUS ... ... **3/6** — —
THE CONSECRATION OF THE BANNER **1/6** — —
  IN THE FOREST (Male voices) ... ... **1/6** — —
PSYCHE **3/0** 7/0
THE DEATH OF YOUNG ROMILLY ... **1/6** — —
THE HESPERUS (Sol-fa, 0/9) ... ... **1/6** — —

DOUGLAS REDMAN.

COR UNAM, VIA UNA ... ... **2/6** — —

C. T. REYNOLDS.

CHILDHOOD OF SAMUEL (Sol-fa, 1/0) ... **2/0** — —

ARTHUR RICHARDS.

PUNCH AND JUDY (Operetta) (Sol-fa, 0/6)... **1/6** — —

J. V. ROBERTS.

JONAH ... ... **2/0** — —

W. S. ROCKSTRO.

THE GOOD SHEPHERD ... ... **2/6** — —

J. L. ROECKEL.

THE SILVER PENNY (Sol-fa, 0/9) ... ... **2/0** — —
THE HOURS (Female voices (Sol-fa, 0/9)) ... **2/0** — —

EDMUND ROGERS.

THE FOREST FLOWER (Female voices) ... **2/6** — —

ROLAND ROGERS.

PRAYER AND PRAISE ... ... **4/0** — —
FLORABEL (Female voices) (Sol-fa, 1/0) ... **2/6** — —

ROMBERG.

THE LAY OF THE BELL (New Edition, translated by the Rev. J. Troutbeck, D.D.) (Sol-fa, 0/8) ... **1/0** 1/6 2/6
THE TRANSIENT AND THE ETERNAL **1/6** — —
  (Ditto, Sol-fa, 0/½)

ROSSINI.

STABAT MATER (Sol-fa, 1/0) **1/0** 1/6 2/6
MOSES IN EGYPT **4/0** 4/6 7/6

CHARLES B. RUTENBER.

DIVINE LOVE ... ... **2/6** — —

ED. SACHS.

WATER LILIES ... ... **1/0** — —

C. SAINTON-DOLBY.

FLORIMEL (Female voices) ... ... **2/6** — —

CAMILLE SAINT-SAËNS.

THE HEAVENS DECLARE—CŒLI ENARRANT **1/6** — —
  (19th Psalm)...

W. H. SANGSTER.

ELYSIUM ... ... **1/0** — —

FRANK J. SAWYER.

THE STAR IN THE EAST ... ... **2/6** — —
THE SOUL'S FORGIVENESS ... ... **1/0** — —

H. W. SCHARTAU.

CHRISTMAS HOLIDAYS (Female voices) ... **0/9** — —

SCHUBERT.

MASS, IN A FLAT **1/0** 1/6 2/6
COMMUNION SERVICE, ditto **2/0** 2/6 4/0
MASS, IN B FLAT **1/0** 1/6 2/6
COMMUNION SERVICE, ditto **2/0** 2/6 4/0
MASS, IN B FLAT **1/0** 1/6 2/6
COMMUNION SERVICE, ditto ... ... **1/0** 1/6 —
MASS, IN C **1/0** 1/6 2/6
COMMUNION SERVICE, ditto **2/0** 2/6 4/0
MASS, IN G **1/0** 1/6 2/6
COMMUNION SERVICE, ditto ... ... **1/0** 1/6 —
MASS, IN F (Sol-fa, 0/9) **2/0** 2/6 4/0
COMMUNION SERVICE, ditto **2/0** 2/6 4/0
SONG OF MIRIAM (Sol-fa, 0/6) ... ... **1/0** — —

SCHUMANN.

THE MINSTREL'S CURSE ... ... **1/6** — —
THE KING'S SON ... ... **1/6** — —
MIGNON'S REQUIEM ... ... **1/0** — —
PARADISE AND THE PERI (Sol-fa, 1/6) ... **1/6** 3/0 6/0
PILGRIMAGE OF THE ROSE... ... ... **1/6** 3/0 —
MANFRED **3/0** 3/6 6/0
FAUST ... ... **3/0** — —
ADVENT HYMN, "In Lowly Guise" ... **1/0** — —
NEW YEAR'S SONG (Sol-fa, 0/6) ... ... **1/0** — —
THE LUCK OF EDENHALL (Male voices) ... **1/6** — —

H. SCHÜTZ.

THE PASSION OF OUR LORD ... ... **1/0** — —

BERTRAM LUARD SELBY.

CHORUSES AND INCIDENTAL MUSIC TO
  "HELENA IN TROAS" ... ... **3/6** — —
SUMMER BY THE SEA (Female voices) ... **1/6** — —
THE WAITS OF BREMEN (For Children) ... **1/6** — —
  Ditto, Sol-fa, 0/6)

H. R. SHELLEY.

VEXILLA REGIS (The Royal Banners forward go) **2/6** — —

E. SILAS.

MASS, IN C	1/0	—	—
COMMUNION SERVICE, IN C	1/6	—	—
JOASH	4/0	—	—

R. SLOMAN.

SUPPLICATION AND PRAISE	2/6	—	—
CONSTANTIA	2/6	—	—

HENRY SMART.

KING RENÉ'S DAUGHTER (Female voices)	2/6	—	—
THE BRIDE OF DUNKERRON (Sol-fa, 1/6)	2/0	2/6	4/0

J. M. SMIETON.

KING ARTHUR (Sol-fa, 1/0)	2/6	—	—
ARIADNE (Sol-fa, 0/9)	2/0	—	—
CONNLA	2/6	—	—

ALICE MARY SMITH.

THE RED KING (Men's voices)	1/0	—	—
THE SONG OF THE LITTLE BALTUNG (ditto) (Ditto, Sol-fa, 0/9)	1/0	—	—
ODE TO THE NORTH-EAST WIND	1/0	—	—
ODE TO THE PASSIONS	2/0	—	—

E. M. SMYTH.

MASS, IN D	2/6	—	—

A. SOMERVELL.

MASS, IN C MINOR	2/6	—	—
THE POWER OF SOUND (Sol-fa, 1/0)	2/0	—	—
THE FORSAKEN MERMAN	1/6	—	—
THE ENCHANTED PALACE (Sol-fa, 0/9)	2/0	—	—
THE CHARGE OF THE LIGHT BRIGADE (Sol-fa, 0/6)	0/9	—	—
ELEGY	1/6	—	—

CHARLTON T. SPEER.

THE DAY DREAM	2/0	—	—
THE JACKDAW OF RHEIMS	2/0	—	—

SPOHR.

MASS (for 5 solo voices and double choir)	2/0	—	—
HYMN TO ST. CECILIA	1/0	—	—
CALVARY	2/0	3/0	4/0
FALL OF BABYLON	2/0	3/6	5/0
LAST JUDGMENT (Sol-fa, 1/0)	1/0	1/6	2/6
THE CHRISTIAN'S PRAYER	1/0	1/6	2/0
GOD, THOU ART GREAT (Sol-fa, 0/6)	1/0	—	—
HOW LOVELY ARE THY DWELLINGS FAIR	0/4	—	—
JEHOVAH, LORD OF HOSTS	0/4	—	—

JOHN STAINER.

THE CRUCIFIXION (Sol-fa, 0/8)	1/6	2/0	—
ST. MARY MAGDALEN (Sol-fa, 1/0)	2/0	2/6	4/0
THE DAUGHTER OF JAIRUS (Sol-fa, 0/9)	1/6	2/0	—

C. VILLIERS STANFORD.

EDEN	5/0	6/0	7/6
THE VOYAGE OF MAELDUNE	2/6	3/0	4/0
CARMEN SÆCULARE	1/6	—	—
THE REVENGE (Sol-fa, 0/9)	1/6	—	—
GOD IS OUR HOPE (46th Psalm)	2/0	—	—
OEDIPUS REX (Male voices)	2/0	—	—
THE EUMENIDES	2/0	—	—
MASS, IN G MAJOR	2/6	—	—
COMMUNION SERVICE, IN G	2/6	—	—
EAST TO WEST	1/6	—	—
THE BATTLE OF THE BALTIC	1/6	—	—

F. R. STATHAM.

VASCO DA GAMA	2/0	—	—

H. W. STEWARDSON.

GEDEON	4/0	—	—

BRUCE STEANE.

THE ASCENSION	2/6	3/6	4/0

J. STORER.

THE TOURNAMENT	2/0	—	—
MASS OF OUR LADY OF RANSOM	2/0	—	—

E. C. SUCH.

NARCISSUS AND ECHO	2/0	—	—
GOD IS OUR REFUGE (46th Psalm)	1/6	—	—

ARTHUR SULLIVAN.

THE GOLDEN LEGEND (Sol-fa, 2/0)	2/6	4/0	5/0
ODE FOR THE COLONIAL AND INDIAN EXHIBITION	1/0	—	—
FESTIVAL TE DEUM	1/0	1/6	2/6

W. TAYLOR.

ST. JOHN THE BAPTIST	—	4/0	—

A. GORING THOMAS.

THE SUN-WORSHIPPERS	1/0	—	—

E. H. THORNE.

BE MERCIFUL UNTO ME	1/0	—	—

BERTHOLD TOURS.

A FESTIVAL ODE	1/0	—	—
THE HOME OF TITANIA (Female voices) (Ditto, Sol-fa, 0/6)	1/6	—	—

FERRIS TOZER.

KING NEPTUNE'S DAUGHTER (Female voices) (Ditto, Sol-fa, 0/6)	2/0	—	—
BALAAM AND BALAK	2/6	—	—

P. TSCHAÏKOWSKY.

NATURE AND LOVE	1/0	—	—

VAN BREE.

ST. CECILIA'S DAY (Sol-fa, 0/9)	1/0	1/6	2/6

CHARLES VINCENT.

THE VILLAGE QUEEN (Female voices)(Sol-fa,0/6)	2/6	—	—
THE LITTLE MERMAID (Female voices)	2/6	—	—

A. L. VINGOE.

THE MAGICIAN (Operetta) (Sol-fa, 0/9)	2/6	—	—

W. S. VINNING.

SONG OF THE PASSION (according to St. John)	1/6	—	—

S. P. WADDINGTON.

JOHN GILPIN	2/6	—	—

W. M. WAIT.

THE GOOD SAMARITAN	2/0	—	—
GOD WITH US	2/0	—	—
ST. ANDREW	2/0	—	—

R. H. WALTHEW.

THE PIED PIPER OF HAMELIN	2/0	—	—

H. W. WAREING.

THE WRECK OF THE HESPERUS	1/6	—	—

WEBER.

IN CONSTANT ORDER (Hymn)	1/6	—	—
MASS, IN G (Latin and English)	1/0	1/6	2/6
MASS, IN E FLAT (Ditto)	1/0	1/6	2/6
COMMUNION SERVICE, IN E FLAT	1/6	—	—
JUBILEE CANTATA	1/0	1/6	—
PRECIOSA	1/0	—	—
THREE SEASONS	1/0	—	—

S. WESLEY.

IN EXITU ISRAEL	0/4	—	—
DIXIT DOMINUS	1/0	—	—

S. S. WESLEY.

O LORD, THOU ART MY GOD	1/0	—	—

J. E. WEST.

SEED-TIME AND HARVEST (Sol-fa, 1/0)	2/6	—	—

C. LEE WILLIAMS.

THE LAST NIGHT AT BETHANY (Sol-fa, 1/0)	2/0	2/6	—
GETHSEMANE	2/0	2/6	—
A HARVEST SONG OF PRAISE	1/6	—	—

A. E. WILSHIRE.

GOD IS OUR HOPE (Psalm 46)	2/0	—	—

THOMAS WINGHAM.

TE DEUM (Latin)	1/6	—	—
MASS, IN D (Regina Cœli)	2/0	—	—

CHAS. WOOD.

ODE TO THE WEST WIND	1/0	—	—

F. C. WOODS.

KING HAROLD (Sol-fa, 0/9)	1/6	—	—
A GREYPORT LEGEND (1797) (Sol-fa, 0/6)	1/6	—	—

E. M. WOOLLEY.

THE CAPTIVE SOUL	2/6	—	—

J. M. W. YOUNG.

THE RETURN OF ISRAEL TO PALESTINE	2/6	3/0	

LONDON & NEW YORK: NOVELLO, EWER AND CO.

THE VILLAGE ORGANIST

A Series of Pieces for Church and General Use

EDITED BY

J. STAINER AND F. CUNNINGHAM WOODS.

PRICE ONE SHILLING EACH BOOK.

Books 1 to 6, elegantly bound in one Vol., cloth, 6s. ; Books 7 to 12, elegantly bound in one Vol., cloth, 6s.

PREFACE.

THIS Collection has been specially compiled with a view to supplying a want felt by the many organists who have only a small instrument at their disposal in country churches, and who often have some difficulty in finding short and easy Voluntaries suitable for their own use and the instruction of their pupils.

To be continued.

LONDON & NEW YORK: NOVELLO, EWER AND CO.

THE
CATHEDRAL PRAYER BOOK

BEING THE

BOOK OF COMMON PRAYER

WITH THE MUSIC NECESSARY FOR THE USE OF CHOIRS

TOGETHER WITH THE

CANTICLES AND PSALTER

POINTED FOR CHANTING

EDITED BY

SIR JOHN STAINER, M.A., Mus. Doc., Oxon.
(Professor of Music in the University of Oxford)

AND

THE REV. WILLIAM RUSSELL, M.A., Mus. Bac., Oxon.
(Succentor of St. Paul's Cathedral).

EXTRACT FROM EDITORS' PREFACE.

THE inconvenience and costliness of the number of separate Books usually requisite for the members of a Choir, in the performance of an ordinary Choral Service, have long pointed to the desirableness of a manual which should, as far as possible, unite under one cover all that is necessary for the choral rendering of, at least, those portions of the Church's Services which are less liable to variation.

The Music of the Versicles and Responses—Festal as well as Ferial—a Psalter and Canticles pointed for chanting, are almost indispensable for the careful and accurate rendering of a Choral Service. And yet, hitherto, it has been scarcely possible to procure these, unless in separate numbers; involving not only much additional expense, but also the disadvantage arising from the continual shifting of books during Service time, which is such a hindrance to a devout participation in Divine Worship.

To remedy these evils, and to assist in promoting, as it is hoped, a more careful and reverent performance of the Divine Offices, the Cathedral Prayer Book has been compiled.

The Editors are fully aware that they are not the first to make an effort in this direction. But they believe that several circumstances have tended to favour their attempt, and ensure its success, which have been wanting in other instances.

This manual provides not only for the daily Morning and Evening Prayer, and the choral celebration of the Holy Communion, in all its completeness, but also for the whole of the occasional Offices contained in the Book of Common Prayer. A special feature of it, moreover, is that it includes an Appendix, in which are contained not only Tallis's Festival Responses and Litany, but a great deal of other additional and miscellaneous matter which it is conjectured will add greatly to its usefulness and value.

The Versicles and Responses throughout the Book (exclusive of the Appendix) and the Litany are from the arrangement used in St. Paul's Cathedral (Stainer and Martin, founded on Goss). They follow Merbecke, although with one or two slight variations which have become traditional in the Cathedral of the Metropolis, and, more recently, in many other Churches.

The Music to the Order for the Administration of the Holy Communion follows the Edition of Merbecke given in "A Choir Book of the Office of Holy Communion" (Stainer), and published some years since. The Order for the Burial of the Dead has also been arranged from Merbecke by the same Editor.

The pointing of the Psalms and Canticles is after that known as the Cathedral Psalter, edited by the Rev. S. Flood-Jones, the late Mr. James Turle, Dr. Troutbeck, Sir John Stainer, and Sir Joseph Barnby. An Edition can also be had in which the Cathedral Psalter Chants to the Canticles and the Psalms are included.

EDITIONS.

The Clergy can be supplied with copies, in quantities of not less than 25, on liberal terms.

LONDON & NEW YORK: NOVELLO, EWER AND CO.

TO CHORAL SOCIETIES.

SHORT CANTATAS

RECENTLY PUBLISHED.

	s. d.
A. Davidson Arnott. — " Young Lochinvar." Ballad for Chorus and Orchestra. Poem by Sir WALTER SCOTT ... ... Tonic Sol-fa, 6d.	1 6
Ethel M. Boyce. — " Young Lochinvar." Ballad by Sir WALTER SCOTT. Set to Music for Baritone Solo, Chorus, and Orchestra ...	1 6
Arthur E. Dyer. — " Saviour of the World " (Salvator Mundi). A Sacred Cantata. Words by FREDERICK E. WEATHERLY, M.A. ...	2 6
Edward Elgar. — " The Black Knight." Cantata for Chorus and Orchestra. The Poem by UHLAND ; translated by LONGFELLOW ...	2 0
Edward Elgar. — " The Light of Life " (Lux Christi). Short Oratorio for Soli, Chorus, and Orchestra. Words by Rev. E. CAPEL-CURE, M.A.	2 6
Alan Gray. — " The Legend of the Rock-Buoy Bell." Ballad for Chorus and Orchestra. Words by SUSAN K. PHILLIPS ...	1 0
F. Kilvington Hattersley. — " Robert of Sicily." Cantata for Soli, Chorus, and Orchestra. Poem by LONGFELLOW	2 6
Oliver King. — " The Sands o' Dee." Ballad for Chorus and Orchestra. Words by CHARLES KINGSLEY	1 0
Oliver King. — " The Romance of the Roses." Cantata for Soprano and Tenor Soli, Chorus, and Orchestra. Words by ELLIS WALTON	2 6

	s. d.
Ed. Sachs. — " Water Lilies." A Fairy Song by FELICIA HEMANS. Deutsche Uebertragung von L. KLEIN	1 0
Arthur Somervell. — " The Forsaken Merman." Cantata for Bass Solo, Chorus, and Orchestra. Words by MATTHEW ARNOLD ...	1 6
William H. Speer. — " The Jackdaw of Rheims." For Chorus and Small Orchestra. Words written by RICHARD BARHAM... ...	2 0
Charles Villiers Stanford. — " East to West." An Ode by ALGERNON CHARLES SWINBURNE. Set to Music for Chorus and Orchestra ...	1 6
S. P. Waddington. — " John Gilpin." Ballad for Chorus and Orchestra. Words selected from COWPER'S poem	2 0
Richard H. Walthew. — " The Pied Piper of Hamelin." By ROBERT BROWNING. Set to Music for Tenor and Bass Soli, Chorus, and Orchestra	2 0
F. Cunningham Woods. — " King Harold." Historical Cantata for Soprano and Tenor Soli and Chorus, with Pianoforte (or Organ) Accompaniment. Words by Rev. C. KENT Tonic Sol-fa, 9d.	1 6
E. M. Woolley. — " The Captive Soul." Cantata for Soprano, Mezzo-Soprano, Contralto, and Tenor Soli, and Chorus of Female voices. Words written by ETHEL C. PEDLEY ...	2 6

CANTATAS FOR FEMALE VOICES.

	s. d.
J. F. Barnett. — " The Wishing Bell." Cantata for Ladies' Voices and Orchestra. Words by JETTA VOGEL ... ... Tonic Sol-fa, 1s.	2 6
E. M. Boyce. — " The Sands of Corriemie." Cantata. Words by E. M. BOYCE ...	1 6
Frederic H. Cowen. — " Summer on the River." The Words written by SHAPCOTT WENSLEY Tonic Sol-fa, 9d.	2 0
Frederic H. Cowen. — " Village Scenes." Words by CLIFTON BINGHAM ... ... Tonic Sol-fa, 9d.	1 6
Frederic H. Cowen. — " The Rose of Life." Words by CLIFTON BINGHAM ... ... Tonic Sol-fa, 9d.	2 0
Frederic H. Cowen. — " A Daughter of the Sea." Words by CLIFTON BINGHAM... ... ... Tonic Sol-fa, 1s.	2 0
J. Maude Crament. — " Little Red-Riding Hood." The Words by J. FREDERICK ROWBOTHAM...	2 0

	s. d.
Myles B. Foster. — " Snow Fairies." Words by SHAPCOTT WENSLEY	1 6
Myles B. Foster. — " The Coming of the King." Words by HELEN M. BURNSIDE ... ... Tonic Sol-fa, 8d.	1 6
A. R. Gaul. — " Around the Winter Fire." Words by SHAPCOTT WENSLEY ... ... Tonic Sol-fa, 9d.	2 0
Battison Haynes. — " A Sea Dream." Cantata for Ladies' Voices, with Recitation (Accompanied). Words by SHAPCOTT WENSLEY ..	2 0
J. L. Roeckel. — " The Hours." Words by SHAPCOTT WENSLEY... ... ... Tonic Sol-fa, 9d.	2 0
B. Luard Selby. — " Summer by the Sea." Written by SHAPCOTT WENSLEY	1 6
Berthold Tours. — " The Home of Titania." Words by SHAPCOTT WENSLEY ... ... Tonic Sol-fa, 6d.	1 6

LONDON & NEW YORK : NOVELLO, EWER AND CO.

28/10/96

www.ingramcontent.com/pod-product-compliance
Lightning Source LLC
Chambersburg PA
CBHW022026080426
42733CB00007B/742

9 7 8 3 7 4 1 1 5 6 1 7 5